CHRISTMAS CHAOS

HIDDEN PICTURE PUZZLES

BY
JILL KALZ

ILLUSTRATED BY
JAMES YAMASAKI

PICTURE WINDOW BOOKS
* a capstone imprint

DESIGNER: LORI BYE
ART DIRECTOR: NATHAN GASSMAN
PRODUCTION SPECIALIST: DANIELLE CEMINSKY
THE ILLUSTRATIONS IN THIS BOOK WERE CREATED DIGITALLY.

PICTURE WINDOW BOOKS
1710 ROE CREST DRIVE
NORTH MANKATO, MN 56003
WWW.CAPSTONEPUB.COM

Library of Congress Cataloging-in-Publication Data
Kalz, Jill.
  Christmas chaos : hidden picture puzzles / by Jill Kalz ;
illustrated by James Yamasaki.
     p. cm. — (Seek it out)
  Summary: "Illustrated scenes related to Christmas and
winter invite readers to find a list of objects hidden within
them"—Provided by publisher.
  ISBN 978-1-4048-7494-7 (library binding)
  ISBN 978-1-4048-7724-5 (paperback)
  ISBN 978-1-40487-991-1 (ebook PDF)
  1. Picture puzzles—Juvenile literature.
I. Yamasaki, James, ill. II. Title.
  GV1507.P47K34 2013
  793.73—dc23
                        2012005225

Printed in the United States of America in
Stevens Point, Wisconsin.
102012   007005R

DIRECTIONS:

Look at the pictures and find the items on the lists. Not too tough, right? Not for a clever kid like you. But be warned: The first few puzzles are tricky. The next ones are even trickier. And the final puzzles are for the bravest seekers only. Good luck!

TABLE OF CONTENTS

penguin

Mrs. Claus

dollhouse

backpack

angel

tricycle

5

Go-Go Snow

deer

rabbit

Santa

toboggan

snowman

snowshoes

7

Cookie Crunch

- marble
- heart
- jingle bell
- wreath
- snowflake
- mitten

I See Ice

- chainsaw
- snow cone
- ladder
- bench
- lost mitten
- bucket of water

10

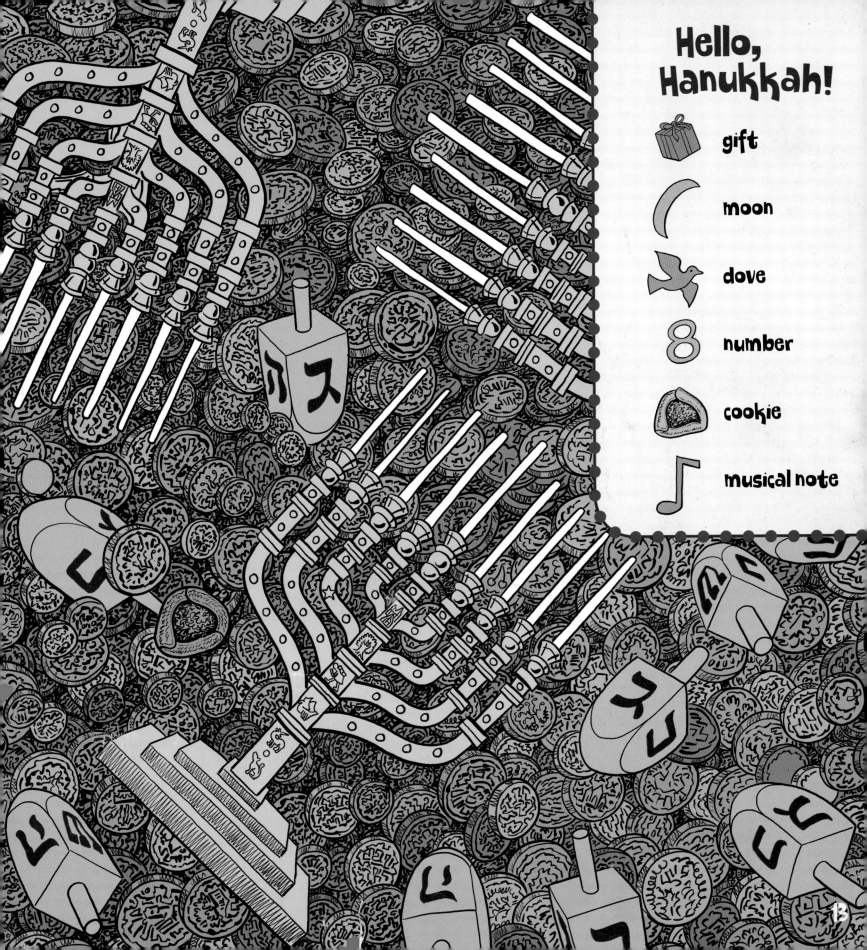

Hello, Hanukkah!

gift

moon

dove

number

cookie

musical note

Icy Delights

- snow shovel
- snowflake
- thermometer
- fish
- dog
- skis
- penguin
- fox
- snow angel

A Merry Morning

snowman

nutcracker

pig

airplane

mouse

dog bone

football

strawberry

elf

16

Night lights

- **words**
- **red-nosed reindeer**
- **gingerbread man**
- **apple**
- **candle**
- **rocking horse**
- **stocking**
- **candy cane**
- **pineapple**

Colorful Kwanzaa

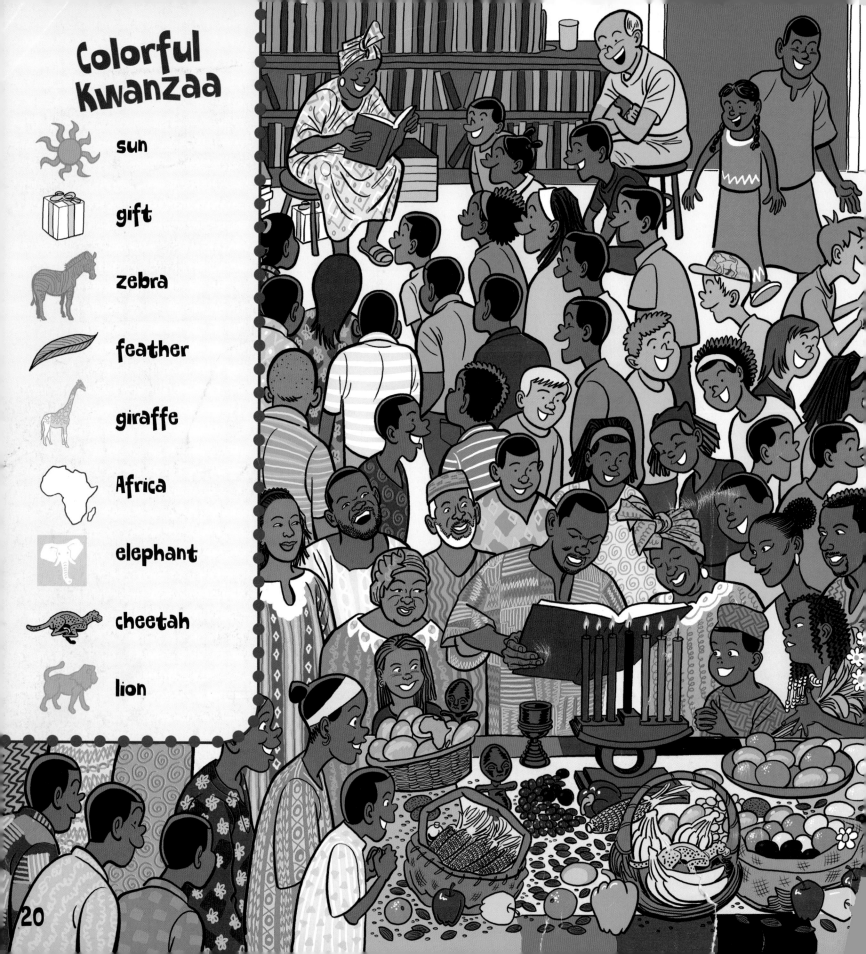

- sun
- gift
- zebra
- feather
- giraffe
- Africa
- elephant
- cheetah
- lion

20

Cool Yule

- pineapple
- mistletoe
- visor
- snowglobe
- dolphin
- holly
- owl
- inner tube
- sweater

23

Clever Elves

 airplane

 bag of coal

 yo-yo

 bicycle

 cookies

 kitten

 fishing pole

 ornament

 reindeer

 mouse

 train

 Mrs. Claus' glasses

25

Ginger Joy

 bow tie

 poinsettia

 heart

 mug

 mailbox

 cherry

 wreath

 hat

 glasses

 stocking

 ribbon

 button

26

27

Cheers for New Year's

 pizza

 bell

 coffee cup

 pine tree

 apple

 candy cane

 hamburger

 ring

 flag

 lion

 Statue of Liberty

 dice

Ho-Ho Holiday

 striped beach towel

 sunscreen

 conch shell

 flag

 crab

 snorkel and mask

 iguana

 camera

 sailboat

 shark fin

 Frisbee

life vest

FOUND EVERYTHING?

Not quite! Flip back and see if you can find these sneaky items.

car

lizard

T. rex

hot-air balloon

cupcake

ostrich

flag

ginger bear

mermaid

pelican

Internet Sites

FactHound offers a safe, fun way to find Internet sites related to this book. All of the sites on FactHound have been researched by our staff.

Here's all you do:

Visit *www.facthound.com*

Type in this code: 9781404874947

Super-cool stuff! Check out projects, games and lots more at **www.capstonekids.com**

Look for all the books in the series:

CHRISTMAS CHAOS

HALLOWEEN HIDE AND SEEK

SCHOOL SHAKE-UP

ZOO HIDEOUT

32